Can democratically elected leaders become dictators?

Here is a well-known example of how a democratically elected government, through a series of clever moves, was able to end democracy, with far-reaching consequences.

In 1928, Adolf Hitler was the leader of the tiny Nazi Party in Germany, with only 12 seats in parliament. Then, in 1933, he was elected Chancellor of Germany with 230 seats. And from Chancellor he became a dictator within a matter of months.

Hitler used the excuse of a fire in the parliament building (the Reichstag) to pass the Reichstag Fire Decree, which suspended most civil liberties in Germany. He whipped up fear by insisting that the fire was the start of a Communist plot to take over Germany. Then a few months later he was able to pass a law called the Enabling Act.

The Act was a special law that gave the Chancellor the power to pass laws by decree, without the involvement of the parliament. He was able to get the law passed in parliament by preventing – through arrests and intimidation – a large enough number of members of parliament from voting. In this way Hitler effectively abolished democracy and established himself as a dictator.

THiNK about

Find out why the Nazi Party became popular in Germany in the late 1920s and early 1930s, and how they came to power. Could something like this happen now, in this or another country?

Adolf Hitler gives the Nazi salute to a group of marching soldiers.

What is justice?

A simple definition of justice is that it is the quality of being fair and reasonable. And fairness means treating everyone equally or in a way that is right or reasonable (although, as we have seen, not everyone agrees on what reasonable means). What we are looking at here is justice as it is formalised in the laws of a country.

One of the most important features of modern democratic societies is the rule of law, which protects the rights of all citizens and limits the power of institutions, business, and even the power of government. Each country has its own justice system and they all work in different ways to implement the rule of law. For example, the justice systems in France, Germany, Italy and the United States, among many others, are very different from the one in the UK.

Why do we send people to prison?

What is the main purpose of sending law-breakers to prison? Is it to rehabilitate them – help them get back to normal life after they've served their time – or simply to punish them? Those who believe that prisons should rehabilitate people say that it will make society safer. Those who focus on punishment are more concerned that the person 'repay a debt to society'.

The rule of law

This is a system of rules developed and agreed over time by the governing body in a country – such as Parliament in the UK or Congress in the US – which apply to all citizens. The rule of law places limits on the power of government, institutions and business and if anyone goes beyond these limits they are penalised or punished.

The main elements of the rule of law in liberal democracies are:

- All citizens are equal under the law. No one may be discriminated against on the basis of their race, religion, ethnic group or gender.
- No one may be arbitrarily – randomly – arrested, imprisoned or exiled.
- Torture and cruel and inhumane treatment are forbidden.
- If a person is detained, they have the right to know the charges against them, and to be presumed innocent until proven guilty according to the law.
- Anyone charged with a crime has the right to a fair and public trial by an impartial (unbiased) court (with competent, ethical and independent representatives).

  No ruler, minister, political party or other group can influence a judge's decision.
- Those in office cannot use their power to enrich themselves.
- No one may be taxed or prosecuted except by a law established in advance.
- No one is above the law, whatever their position in society.
- The law is fairly, impartially and consistently enforced by courts that are independent of the other branches of government and other groups.

A cell from the prison on Alcatraz Island California, USA, which was operational between 1934 and 1963, and is now a museum. Alcatraz was a high-security prison, and the emphasis was on punishment rather than rehabilitation.

"The prison system needs to be beneficial for the prisoners for the sake of their victims. If you are in there [prison] fighting for your life, you are not going to be able to get the new skills needed to make you more likely to succeed as a law-abiding citizen."

Erwin James, editor of a newspaper for people in prison. While himself in prison for murder, he was helped by a prison psychologist to 'feel human', and to 'understand the importance of moral values'.

What happens when the law gets it wrong?

Miscarriages of justice happen when mistakes, deliberate or otherwise, are made in the process of charging and taking someone through the criminal justice system. The mistakes can be made by the police, lawyers, witnesses, judges or juries; sometimes people make up evidence or simply lie. So, innocent people are sometimes convicted of crimes. These miscarriages of justice can take many years to put right, and some may never be.

Stefan Kiszko was one tragic victim of a miscarriage of justice. He was convicted of the murder of a 16-year-old girl, and spent 16 years in prison, until a campaign showed that he could not have committed the murder. The serious mistakes included the police not following up important evidence which would immediately have proved his innocence, and that three teenage girls lied in court.

The fact that miscarriages of justice can and do happen is considered by many the strongest argument against the death penalty.

THINK about

What do you think should be the purpose of imprisoning someone?

What's the difference between prejudice and discrimination?

Prejudice is an unfair and unreasonable opinion or feeling, especially when formed without much thought or knowledge (the word prejudice means to pre-judge). It often leads to discrimination, which has been described as 'prejudice with power'. Discrimination means treating a person or particular group of people differently – especially in a worse way from the way in which other people are treated – because of their skin colour, sex, sexuality, disability, ethnicity, religious or other beliefs, or other attributes.

Throughout history

Prejudice and discrimination have been commonplace throughout human history. People in societies and groups have a tendency to identify with their own group. People can also be suspicious or fearful of those who belong to other groups. This can range from small groups to whole societies, and in its worst form the suspicion can become xenophobia (from two Greek words meaning 'foreign' and 'fear').

Changing society

In the past, discrimination was often built into laws in society. For example, in the nineteenth century, Roman Catholics weren't allowed to hold any public positions in Britain. But as social attitudes change, laws are changed, and it becomes unacceptable and unlawful to discriminate against certain groups.

You can see this most clearly in Great Britain in the way the laws relating to homosexuality have changed. Until 1967, homosexual acts between men were a criminal offence. (Apparently, lesbians either didn't exist or they were exempt!)

There were a number of other changes, until in 2010 the Equality Act was passed (see panel), and in 2013 and 2014 laws were passed in England and Wales, and Scotland, which allowed same-sex marriage. (Northern Ireland still doesn't recognise same-sex marriage.)

Equality Act 2010

This UK Act of Parliament made it illegal to discriminate against anyone because of their gender, disability, race, religion or belief, sexual orientation or age.

Hate crime has now been added to legislation, and people are encouraged to report any incidents to the police. A hate incident is 'any incident which the victim, or anyone else, thinks is based on someone's prejudice towards them because of their race, religion, sexual orientation, disability or because they are transgender'.

Stereotypes

A stereotype is a widely held, but inflexible and oversimplified view of a particular type of person or thing. Some stereotyping, for example, that Welsh people are good at singing, might be thought to be harmless, but sometimes the stereotype can be really damaging. For example, if a certain group of people are stereotyped as not as being as clever as everyone else, how does this affect the way that institutions treat those people? Look at the way that stereotypes affected Richard Rieser as he was growing up (pages 22-23).

How do mutual respect and tolerance work in a multi-cultural society?

How can a society balance toleration of the beliefs and practices of people from different cultures or religions living within it, when some of the practices might contradict the values expressed in the laws of that country? For example, bigamy is against the law in the UK, but isn't in all countries. Can you think of any other laws like this?

What's the best way of dealing with any real differences? Do we really know about different practices, or do we have a stereotyped view of the values and practices of other groups?

THINK about

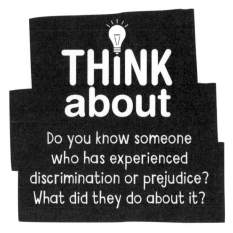

Do you know someone who has experienced discrimination or prejudice? What did they do about it?

Demonstrators protest against a Russian law banning gay 'propaganda'. In 2017, the European court of human rights ruled that such laws were 'incompatible with the notions of equality, pluralism and tolerance inherent in a democratic society'.

My experience

Richard Rieser

Richard Rieser was born in 1948. He is the managing director of World of Inclusion Ltd, a company that works to promote equality for disabled people, and an international equality trainer, consultant, film maker, writer and teacher.

He told us about how his experiences of prejudice and discrimination influenced his ideas about what is right and wrong.

Included and excluded

I caught polio at nine months: I lost power in the muscles of my left leg, my chest, back and right arm. My parents were keen for me to do everything that everyone else did. I could swim, ride a bike and walk with a limp. It was the 1950s and I was in a gang on our street, climbing trees and playing on bombsites.

The first act of discrimination against me was when the head of a primary school refused to allow me to go to his school as I was a 'fire-risk'. There were only three steps! This meant that I couldn't go to a school where my friends were.

Experiencing prejudice

Our council, the London County Council, tried to put me into a special school for the 'physically handicapped'. I visited it and it reminded me of the hospital I had been in: all the children in wheelchairs, calipers etc, were sitting around doing nothing. I had a tantrum as I hated it. My parents fought for me to go a mainstream private school, paid for by the Council.

When I was 14, I transferred myself to a local secondary modern school. It was on six floors but I wasn't allowed to use the lift. The other boys bullied and taunted me because of my leg. They told me I was 'ugly' and a 'cripple'. I believed this for years. Some staff joined in with this, especially in PE.

Making sense of the world

I went to university and got a degree in Geography, and I studied for a further degree, too.

I was trying to make sense of the world: I rejected religion as I thought it was hypocritical. I realised that most of the things I had been brought up to believe in, such as patriotism and the pursuit of profits, were wrong. These created poverty and suffering throughout the world. I decided to spend time building community groups, working with trade unions and organising in factories with working class people.

Eventually, I trained as a teacher. My needs as a disabled person weren't met – for example I was teaching in many rooms on different floors. I thought that this was my personal problem, but then I realised that disability was not 'natural' but is created by society, along with discrimination against people because of their nationality, gender, race, sexuality and poverty.

Challenging discrimination

I discovered a whole history of the depiction of disability as generalised and negative: the lame boy in the 'Pied Piper of Hamelin' is the only child left behind; the witch in 'Hansel and Gretel' is blind and walks with a stick; the baddies in 'James Bond' films are usually disabled in some way.

I came to understand that disability is a socially created oppression, which stereotypes all of us with long-term impairments instead of seeing us how we are: equal but different. This led me to develop my thinking about the need for disability equality, especially in schools.

The high point for me was representing the UK Disabled People's Movement at the United Nations. I helped draft the UN Convention on the Rights of Persons with Disabilities.

"We are equal but different."

UN Convention on the Rights of Persons with Disabilities

The Convention was adopted by the United Nations in 2006. It's an international human rights treaty intended to protect the rights and dignity of persons with disabilities.

Parties to the Convention – all the countries that signed it – are required to 'promote, protect, and ensure the full enjoyment of human rights by persons with disabilities, and ensure that they enjoy full equality under the law'.

The Convention is helping to ensure that people with disabilities are seen as full and equal members of society, with the same human rights as everyone else.

THiNK about

What would you do if you saw a disabled person being bullied?

How does fairness and unfairness affect people?

Inequality and poverty

When we talk about inequality we are normally talking about the situation in society where some people have much more money and many more opportunities than other people. Is this situation fair? Is it fair that there are poor people in society – with little money and few possessions, while others have lots more money and many more opportunities? Not everyone would say this was unfair, so it's important to think about this.

A homeless person sleeps on the street in Paris, France.

Is inequality bad for society?

Many people believe that it is. There are two arguments put forward for why we should narrow the gap between rich and poor in society. One is simply that huge inequalities are immoral and unjust. The parallel argument is that society should be organised to ensure 'the greatest good for the greatest number'. People who believe this argue that everyone in society should be cared for, that people should not be allowed to fall into dire poverty, that everyone should have access to health care, a good education and housing, and that this should be paid for through taxation, in particular a system of progressive income tax – where the wealthy are taxed at higher rates.

Some people don't agree that inequality is a problem. They oppose the redistribution of wealth through taxing the wealthy at higher rates, and agree with Benjamin Franklin, one of the founders of the United States, that giving help to the poor makes them less likely to want to work. They believe that money from the rich will always 'trickle down' to the poor – for example through jobs – and that it's not the responsibility of the government to take care of the poor.

"... I think the best way of doing good to the poor, is not making them easy in poverty, but leading or driving them out of it."

Benjamin Franklin

Are unequal societies 'unhealthy', making them bad for everyone?

There is a great deal of evidence that the economies of very unequal societies are not 'healthy', and unhealthy economies affect everyone negatively. In a purely practical way, when wealth becomes concentrated in the hands of a few people, the majority of people have little spare money to spend on everything from clothes and tech devices to going out for a meal or even buying takeaways. This affects the businesses that provide the goods and services; people lose their jobs, and this makes the economy weak. People who are in the lowest-paid jobs have even less to spend on necessities, and everyone becomes poorer. So an unhealthy economy affects everyone in society.

An attempt to reduce inequality

During and after the Second World War, the government in Britain did its best to reduce inequalities. They recognised that people needed to feel that the significant burdens of the war were shared fairly by everyone. So the rationing of food, clothing and petrol affected everyone. This meant, for example, that everyone was allowed the same amount of meat, butter and sugar. In this way the government was able to ask everyone to participate.

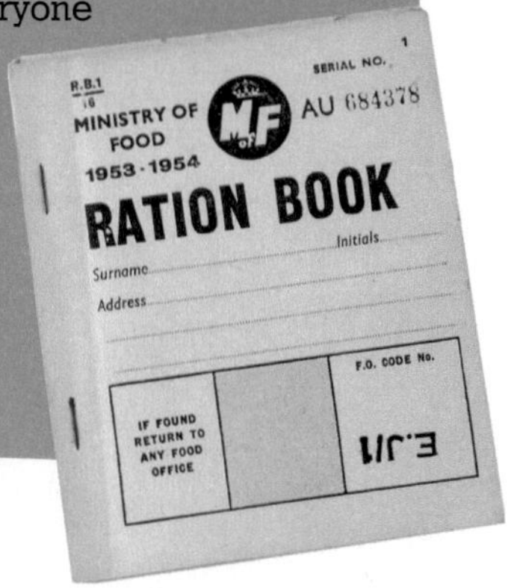

What can be done to change the situation?

It is possible to change the inequalities in society through the policy choices made by governments, and also, on a more local scale, through supporting forms of economic democracy, where employees have a say in how an enterprise is run, and even in how profits are shared. These changes can only come about if enough people in a society decide that it's in everyone's best interests to have greater equality.

"Homelessness and child poverty have risen, the NHS is in dire financial straits, understaffed prisons have record suicide rates, the elderly lack social care – yet the rich continue to get richer, and continue to avoid taxes. This is an expression of abject moral bankruptcy."

Professors Kate Pickett and Richard Wilkinson, writing in *The Guardian* in 2017

THiNK about

Do those who have the wealth have more power? Is that fair?

Is it people's own fault if they are poor?

Should governments provide health care, education and housing for everyone?

How does inequality affect educational opportunity?

Education is not just about what we learn or don't learn. It's also about how education itself is divided up into different routes and pathways. And it's about the kinds of opportunities that parents provide to enable children to 'get on'.

Routes through education

Here are two contrasting routes that people in the UK might take through education into life. We could say that Maria and Robert take route one while Abdul and Leanne take route two.

Route One

- **Maria and Robert are each brought up by a single parent who has had no higher education**
- can't afford nursery
- primary school
- secondary school
- made to move out of the school to a different one, because school thought they wouldn't pass the GCSE exam (and that would affect the school's grades)
- 'training' ie retail apprenticeship
- work in a store
- rented shared accommodation
- benefits subsidising low wages

Route Two

- **Abdul and Leanne are each born into wealth**
- private nursery
- private school
- 'common entrance'
- public school (fee-paying)
- university
- parents' contacts enable child to do internship with parents' support
- parents help pay off university fees and loans
- well-paid job
- parents pay deposit on a house

Can you think of other routes, or other maps?

> "... to educate not according to ability, but according to the social situation of the parents, is both wrong and a waste."
>
> The writer Alan Bennett, speaking at Cambridge University in 2014

Finland

Three decades ago, the government in Finland realised that their education system was seriously failing children, and they decided to make revolutionary changes, including scrapping all testing and not starting formal schooling until the age of seven. They abolished all private schools, so that everyone attends a state school, and they raised the status of teachers through higher pay and by insisting that all teachers have a Master's qualification.

There are day care programmes for babies and toddlers and one year pre-school for six-year-olds, followed by nine years of compulsory comprehensive schooling. Students can then choose between an academic or a vocational track, both of which usually take three years and give a qualification to continue to tertiary education.

After years of no testing at all, Finland decided to see how their education system was doing compared to others. They joined an international testing programme (called PISA – OECD Programme for International Study Assessment) and found they were at the top. They are still consistently high, but recognise that they must keep evolving.

Children in Finland attend school between the ages of seven and 15.

Fairness in education

Ideas about a fair way to run education have changed and they are different in different countries. For example, in 1944 the government for England and Wales introduced an exam at 11 called the 11-plus, which all children took. The ones who passed went to a grammar school, those that failed went to secondary modern schools. Some people also went to technical colleges. At first people thought this was fair but, by the 1960s, most people came to think it wasn't, and so the government introduced comprehensive schools.

Meanwhile, private education was never abolished and some areas kept grammar schools. Some people think this is fair. Some don't. What do you think?

THINK about

Find out what you can about the ideas behind the way education systems are organised in different parts of the world.

Are there fairer systems in other countries?

My experience

Tulip Siddiq

Tulip Siddiq was born in 1982. She is the Labour Party Member of Parliament for Hampstead and Kilburn, and was Shadow Minister for Education (Early Years) between 2016 and 2017. She has worked at Amnesty International and Save the Children on issues related to human trafficking and modern-day slavery. She told us what she thinks about injustice in society and how to combat it.

Is it right to treat people well or badly because they are different in some way?

There is a lot of discrimination against people because of their skin colour, their disabilities, religion, gender and sexuality, to list the most common. In 2015/2016 there were over 169 hate-driven incidents happening in the UK every day, against people who simply look different or have different beliefs from others. For me, it's very important that people from all backgrounds work together to stop prejudice and discrimination.

To take some examples I've seen in my own life: my father uses a wheelchair. Is it right that he faces discrimination in his search for a job because of his physical disability? My mother worships at a mosque and my neighbour at a synagogue. Is it right that they have to deal with the prejudice of people who shout nasty insults at them because of their religious beliefs?

People, like myself, who work in politics, have an extra responsibility to create laws (or acts) that protect those who experience prejudice, because we represent all our constituents. One Act that I'm proud of is the Equality Act 2010 (see page 20), which protects people from discrimination in their workplace and in wider society. This Act entitles everyone, regardless of background, to the same treatment from an employer.

Education is the enemy of prejudice

I believe education is the best way to stop prejudice from developing, and it also works against already established prejudice. I was lucky enough to go to good schools with broad-minded, inclusive teachers. But sadly, not everyone in the world has the same opportunities as I had or that my daughter will have.

There are other benefits to education, too. When people can read and write and discuss issues openly, they are able to understand more, and people from different backgrounds are more accepting of each other, as they learn about each other's cultures in school. Better education also means a better qualified workforce, which allows economies to flourish at home and trade peacefully with one another.

More broadly, those who can, need to work towards a world in which every child can go to school. To make this happen, we need to make sure we keep helping the poorest countries, and ensure that governments spend enough money on education to give every child the best chance of success both here and elsewhere. That will benefit us all.

What else can we do?

You don't have to be a politician to help stop discrimination and prejudice. Bringing people of different faiths, belief systems and cultures together is a really successful way of reducing prejudice. This way, people can share their cultures and reduce the likelihood of division and exclusion.

And events like the Paralympics (right) give athletes a chance to show the entire world that having a disability should be no barrier to ambition and achievement.

Prejudice does not have to exist and by bringing people together and making our vision inclusive, not exclusive, we can help to create a better world for everyone.

Opportunities for education

According to the United Nations, 61 million children of primary school age were not in school in 2016, with girls far less likely than boys to attend school.

However, things are changing. Since 2000, the United Nations says that the number of children who were out of school has fallen by almost half. This is great news. Understanding, through better schooling and education, starves ignorance and prejudice, making us all winners.

"Prejudice does not have to exist."

Is there a right and wrong way to use language?

What part does language play in how we decide what's right and wrong? Are there right and wrong ways to use language? Should we try to control how people write and speak?

These are very complicated questions.

One example

In July 2017, the Member of Parliament Anne Marie Morris was recorded at an event using a particular expression. She said,

"Now we get to the real n----- in the woodpile, which is, in two years what happens if there is no deal?"

You'll see that we've written one of the words as 'n-----'. That's because the word has a history which is tied up with slavery and the idea that some people (millions, actually) could be bought, sold and forced to work. We've reached a point in most parts of the English-speaking world where we think the word is unrepeatable and yet here was an MP in 2017 using it. She apologised and the Prime Minister suspended her.

All this caused a debate in the mainstream media and on social media, too. Some people said that it showed that this MP used the expression regularly without thinking and she moved in circles where people didn't stop her to tell her it was offensive. Others said this was 'over-reacting' and it was 'unintentional', meaning that she didn't mean any harm to anyone.

By 1860 there were four million slaves in the United States. People were bought and sold at markets like this one.

Some language 'sleeps'

Part of the problem is that some unrepeatable words like the 'n word' sit in phrases and old rhymes where they 'sleep'. That's to say, they're not 'actively' being used to describe someone or, say, to order them to do something, which is how that word used to be used. Another problem is that the word hasn't died out everywhere. A good few African-American rappers and comedians use the word, though usually they would say that it was OK for them to use the word, but it's not OK for a white person to use it.

Why would they say that?

Language and power – the staircase

The answer lies in the fact that such language is not 'neutral', it's always used in situations which are already set up in a particular kind of way. This is what's known as the 'language and power' question. Some groups of people in society tend to have more power than other groups. There are 'hierarchies', arranged as on an imaginary staircase. Very few people would say we aren't all somewhere on this staircase. Where people disagree is whether we can all move up (or down) the staircase when we want to or have the ability to.

There's been a huge argument over the last 100 years or so about this and what are the right or wrong things to do about it. One part of that argument is about how we use words to describe each other.

People ask, are white people more likely to be above black people on the staircase? Are there words which not only reflect these positions but have the power to keep people lower than others? That explains why, when African-American rappers use those words, it's 'ironic' – they are mocking the way people have used the word when talking to people lower down. And it's also a way of reclaiming language that was once used to abuse them.

There is the same argument about words to do with any group that experiences prejudice. People from higher up the hierarchy using these words about people lower down helps to create and consolidate the hierarchy. Some people say this use of language is not only offensive, it's using power to create prejudice and discrimination and it has to stop.

> "Language is very powerful. Language does not just describe reality. Language creates the reality it describes."
>
> Archbishop Desmond Tutu

THiNK about

What do you think? Is it ever acceptable to use the 'n word', or other words that have a negative history, even if that word is being 'reclaimed'?

My experience

Laura Bates

Laura Bates was born in 1986. She is the founder of the Everyday Sexism Project, which has gathered over 100,000 testimonies of gender inequality worldwide. Laura writes regularly for several publications, and also works with international groups tackling rape and abuse. We asked her what she thinks about right and wrong in society.

How do ideas of what is right and wrong develop?

Most of us have firm ideas of what is right and wrong, without ever being taught them explicitly. This is especially true in relation to what's considered right and wrong for girls and boys. We've all accepted these ways of judging people depending on their gender, without ever really talking about it. These ideas are often sexist, racist or homophobic, but we internalise them because they're all around us.

For example, we learn from children's toys (dolls for girls, engineering kits for boys) what careers are considered 'suitable' before we're even old enough to walk. Girls get told they're beautiful and boys that they're big and strong. Films and television most often show men doing brave and powerful things and women looking for love or being a sidekick for a man.

What effect does inequality have on people's lives?

I often hear people say that 'everybody has the same chances, and if there are different outcomes to people's lives that's their fault'. But the process of getting to the outcomes depends on your starting point.

If you start with fewer advantages – money, education, expectations – getting to the same outcome as someone with all the advantages is harder, if you can get there at all. There are so many obstacles along the way, including the low expectations of teachers or others, prejudice and lack of funds.

We have to remove the invisible barriers instead of placing blame on the people who are being held back by those barriers.

That goes for all sorts of different situations. For example, girls are told how to dress and behave, and not to go out alone to avoid being assaulted. This puts the onus on girls and young women, and not on those making the decision to do wrong.

So what should we do?

First, recognise that many different sorts of discrimination can be invisible. For example, many people think that sexism doesn't exist any more, and if we are white we may not see racism in action, but this doesn't mean that these problems don't exist. We must recognise the problems before we can start to solve them, so the first thing is to listen to other people's experiences.

The second challenge is to recognise all those stereotypes that sneak in without our realising. For example, sexism in the media – when we hear about the shoes and dresses of female politicians but the policies of their male peers.

We need to campaign for politicians and businesses to make fair policies to tackle inequality and discrimination.

In the Women's March on Washington in January 2017, millions of people showed they were no longer prepared to allow sexism and inequality to continue in silence.

We should all play a part

But most of all, every one of us has to play a part if we want to change what's currently seen as normal. So, for example, if a woman is walking down the street and a man harasses her, a passer by who challenges him would send a powerful message that it's not OK. This doesn't have to involve confrontation. It might just mean offering help or support to the woman. But if we just walk on by we also send a message: this is normal and we don't have a problem with it.

It isn't enough to have strong values and keep quiet about them. We have to speak up when we see injustice, and put our values into action.

THiNK about

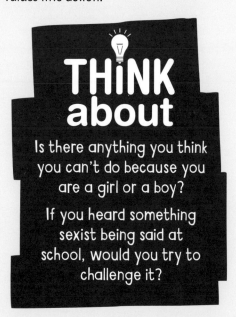

Is there anything you think you can't do because you are a girl or a boy?

If you heard something sexist being said at school, would you try to challenge it?

> **"We have to speak up when we see injustice, and put our values into action."**

How does right and wrong work on a global scale?

Pollution and climate change are global problems

There are some issues, such as pollution and climate change, that have an impact on the welfare of individuals and communities all over the world. Can the problems caused by pollution and climate change be solved by doing what is right and stopping doing what is wrong? That could be a straightforward solution if everyone agreed about what is right and wrong in these situations, but that, of course, isn't the case.

What is pollution?

Pollution is the damage caused to the environment – the water, the air and the land around us – by harmful substances or waste. The increasing population of the world and the resultant demand on resources, and insufficient controls and laws to prevent pollution, have led to an increase in pollution.

What are climate change and global warming?

Global warming refers to the Earth's rising surface temperature, while climate change includes this warming and its effects, such as melting glaciers and the subsequent rise in sea levels, and an increase in extreme weather, leading to flooding or drought.

Global warming is one symptom of the much larger problem of climate change caused by humanity itself, resulting from the rapid increase in carbon dioxide and other greenhouse gases that affect the Earth's atmosphere. Greenhouse gases mostly result from: the burning of fossil fuels (coal, oil and natural gas), solid waste, trees and wood products; certain chemical reactions in manufacture; the methane emissions from livestock; and the transformation of the Earth's landscape, for instance from carbon-storing forests to farmland.

In 2017, a third of Bangladesh was affected by flooding.

How can the problems of pollution and climate change be solved?

These are huge questions and there are no simple answers. But we can only begin to solve these problems by looking at each issue in detail and then deciding what to do in each case; in fact, by deciding what is the right thing to do, and what is the wrong thing.

The only way this will be solved is through world cooperation. It's a matter of balancing different rights – for example, the rights of farmers to put pesticides on their land (polluting the water table and rivers), in order to increase their crop yields, against the rights of everyone to have clean water, free from pesticides.

There are people who say they don't believe the scientists about climate change and its effects. For example, US President Donald Trump (below) supports the coal, oil and car manufacturing industries and doesn't agree with restricting their activities.

THiNK about

Should governments ban all combustion engines, and phase in electric cars? Would that work?

If you had the power, what would you do about climate change?

Balancing harms

It's also a matter of deciding which solutions cause the least harm. For example, when governments and scientists were concentrating on climate change and looking at the effect of carbon emissions, diesel fuel for cars was encouraged because diesel produced fewer carbon emissions. But it's since become clear that diesel cars produce more pollutants which contribute to the air pollution from traffic, and that these pollutants cause serious respiratory illnesses. As a result, governments are considering a number of measures, including introducing penalties for diesel cars and banning them altogether. People who had been encouraged to buy diesel cars say that this is unfair. What should governments do?

Car manufacturers are making changes. too. For example, Volvo recently announced that it will no longer launch new car models powered only by internal combustion engines, and instead will produce only pure electric or hybrid cars, which create less pollution. Other car manufacturers are also now looking at changing over.

But will these measures happen quickly enough?

Find out

Find out what you can about different kinds of renewable energy and nuclear power. What are their advantages and disadvantages?

Is it ever right to go to war?

Are all wars bad and wrong? Are some 'right' or 'necessary'? Who decides? These are very complex questions, and people – including philosophers, theologians and politicians – have always argued about them. War is either offensive – when one country attacks or invades another; or defensive – when a country that has been attacked or invaded defends itself against the attacker, or helps another country that has been attacked. This might sound straightforward, but most situations are not clear-cut.

The question always comes back to fairness. Think about someone who is being bullied. Should they stand up to the bully and fight back in some way? Is that the right, or best, thing to do? Does talking work? Can arguments between two sides – even countries – be settled by discussion and negotiation?

> "War is what happens when language fails."
>
> Margaret Atwood, novelist

Was the Second World War a 'necessary war'?

Most people say that it was, because of the way Hitler's Germany (see page 17) and her allies behaved.

The causes of the war are complex, and go back to the aftermath of Germany's defeat in the First World War. Under the Treaty of Versailles, Germany lost territory to pay for the damage caused by the war. This caused resentment among the German people, as it brought hardship to many. In the early 1930s, the Nazi Party's Adolf Hitler (see page 17) was voted into power after he promised to rip up the hated Treaty. Hitler's programme of retaking lost territory started in 1936 when German troops entered the Rhineland. This was followed by invasions into Sudetenland in Czechoslovakia.

Britain and France did not want to start another war, so they accepted Hitler's assurances that he would stop there. But he didn't. In 1939, he invaded the rest of Czechoslovakia. Still, Britain and France were not prepared to take military action, but they did promise that if Germany invaded Poland they would. This happened in September, 1939. Britain and France were then at war with Germany.

Find out

Find out what you can about Hitler and the Nazis, and their actions, both before the war started and during the war. Do you think it was right to go to war against them?

What if someone disagrees with a war?

According to the UN Convention on Human Rights, a conscientious objector is an 'individual who has claimed the right to refuse to perform military service on the grounds of freedom of thought, conscience, or religion'. The Convention upholds this principle, and supports laws allowing objectors to be exempted from military service altogether, or to serve either as non-combatants or in civilian services.

There wasn't always such a humane attitude, and conscientious objectors have been imprisoned and even executed at different times in history.

Muhammad Ali, conscientious objector

Muhammad Ali, the American boxer and activist (below), in 1966 refused to be conscripted into the armed forces because he was opposed to the Vietnam War. He was denied a boxing licence and was stripped of his passport and heavyweight title; the case against him was overturned on appeal after four years.

The United Nations

The United Nations has discussed and passed many resolutions on issues related to war, invasions and occupations. And in international law it's illegal to invade a country purely and only in order to change the government ('regime change').

A controversial action?

In 2003, the USA and Britain invaded Iraq. They did so to oust Saddam Hussein (regime change) and his government. They claimed that Iraq had 'weapons of mass destruction' and this was sufficient reason. This was never proved and they didn't wait for a second UN resolution before taking action. According to UN statutes, this was an illegal act.

THiNK about

If your country went to war, under what circumstances would you take part?

Find out how people have resisted invasions and occupations. If your country was invaded, under what circumstances would you resist?

How do children learn about right and wrong?

Dos and Don'ts

If you are someone under 18 reading this page, the chances are that the life you lead is full of rules (dos and don'ts), with punishments, sanctions and words of 'rebuke' (ie being told off) if you break them.

It's obvious that for the very first years of your life, if you don't like any of this, there's nothing you can do about it apart from shout – which we've all seen babies and toddlers do very often!

Can you question the rules?

As we get older things change. We start to have all sorts of ideas about right and wrong that might not be exactly the same as our parents' and carers'. These might be to do with, for example, what you're allowed to do (bedtimes, going out, what kinds of friends you have, etc). They might be about the kinds of punishments you get when you break the rules. They can also be about who makes up the rules and whether you get a say in things.

Now let's switch to school. Some of the rules and punishments are similar but some are different, especially to do with when it's not right to talk, when not to get up and walk around, what kinds of punishments are given out for disobeying the rules (being sent to see the headteacher, detentions, suspensions, exclusions, etc).

Pupil Referral Units

What happens to young people who don't or can't abide by the rules? They might be excluded from mainstream school and sent to a Pupil Referral Unit (PRU). These have been designed to provide education for children who are excluded, sick, or for other reasons are unable to attend a mainstream or special school. So, they are not only for children who have been excluded from school because of their behaviour, although many of them are what is called 'challenging'. The best PRUs treat every child as an individual and work with them to help them learn, and enjoy learning.

"It takes time - you have to be there, listen to them rant and so on. The bottom line is trust."... We "increased attendance by 30 per cent by creating an environment where pupils want to be. Every day they come in because the experience is a positive one - they feel welcomed and it's safe."

Tony Meehan, head teacher of Latimer Alternative Provision Academy

Ideas about punishments change

One debate that has taken place many times in the last 50 years is over the physical punishment of children. For example, when Michael Rosen was nine years old in 1955, he booed a teacher in the school playground and was caned with a stick for 'disobedience'. In 1986, physical punishment of school children by teachers was banned by the UK government in state-run schools. Meanwhile a debate goes on as to whether the government should pass a law banning parents and carers from hitting children. There are already laws that ban physical punishment in the home as well as at school in nearly 50 countries (Sweden was the first in 1979), but in the UK it's not yet banned if it's what's described as 'reasonable' punishment.

THiNK about

Some people say that governments are right to abolish physical or corporal punishment in order to protect children. Others argue that it should be nothing to do with government, and should always be the decision of the parents and schools themselves. What do you think?

Find out

See what you can find out about what happens to children under 18 who not only break the rules at school, but also break the law.

This illustration from the 1880s shows how children used to be hit on the hand with a cane as a punishment for disobedience.

My experience

Alex Wheatle

The writer Alex Wheatle was born in 1963 and spent most of his childhood in a Surrey children's home. He received a short prison sentence following the Brixton uprising of 1981. In prison, and after his release, he wrote poems and lyrics, becoming known as the Brixton Bard. He won the 2016 Guardian Children's Fiction Prize and was nominated for the Carnegie Medal in 2016 and 2017. We asked Alex how his experiences have influenced his values and his ideas of what is right and wrong.

What effect did your treatment in the children's home have on you?

When I was three I was sent into the Shirley Oaks care home. It was a place of nightmares, where certain adults physically, sexually and mentally abused children with impunity. To be told your parents abandoned you like you're a bag of rubbish – you believe it. It affects your whole worldview.

Before the age of 18, I felt worthless, and because of this I sabotaged every opportunity I had at school and further education. I was excellent at cricket and was once offered the chance to be captain of the school cricket team. I declined. I shied away from any kind of responsibility. I saw value in others, but not in myself.

Growing up, my notion of right and wrong was confused. I was fulfilling the very worst expectations I had of myself.

How did you develop a sense of self worth?

As a teenager, I struggled with anger and trust issues, left school with no qualifications, slipped into petty crime and then landed in prison for five months following the 1981 Brixton uprising.

The only way I could access love and see value in myself was when someone else did. This gateway happened in prison, when I wrote poems about my life in care. My cell-mate said 'That's very good.' He was a Rastafarian and had a tremendous belief in himself. The recognition from those poems and the self-worth that followed led me, finally, to believe that I could contribute to society.

Sharing a small space with another person meant I had to consider someone else's space and feelings. I slowly came to realise that other people had difficult experiences too, and I wanted to write about their backgrounds and traumas.

What do you think prisons should be for?

I believe that we can help people to develop and change, so we should rehabilitate, not just punish. I came out of prison determined to do something with my life. I began to read greedily and I trained as an engineer. I was also keeping a diary, writing song lyrics and poetry.

Can reading make a difference?

Reading fiction builds empathy. I believe this very strongly. I started to devour books and empathised with the characters. I think that if young people involved in knife crime read stories, they would begin to see themselves in other children, empathy would grow and they would consider laying down their knives. Schools could encourage this.

"I was determined that any child of mine would have love."

How has being a father changed you?

The biggest impact on me was becoming a father at twenty. My own lack of love as a child drove me – I was determined that any child of mine would have love.

It's wrong to look on any set of children and see some as failures, or potential failures.

We need to build esteem and to help all children develop emotionally, as well as educating them intellectually.

We need to reassess the notion of failure. Children are living with stress levels we haven't seen before. Social media highlights what the elites are doing, wearing, what they own. The pressures are on children to do or have the same.

Parents need the support of school and society to help them instil their children with belief in themselves. It is a challenge.

All children should be seen as having equal value and worth

We should be educating all children from a young age that every individual has worth. Society's expectations of those children in care or from poor homes are the lowest. This is wrong.

The poorest child's life should be seen as just as valuable as that of a prince or princess.

THiNK about

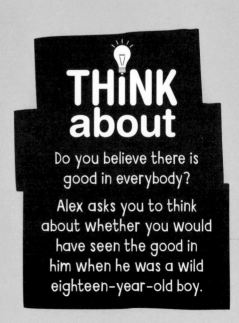

Do you believe there is good in everybody?

Alex asks you to think about whether you would have seen the good in him when he was a wild eighteen-year-old boy.

How do disasters make us question what's right and wrong?

As we all know, every so often there are disasters: floods, fires, traffic pile-ups, gas explosions and many more terrible events. These raise important questions about right and wrong.

- Was the disaster really 'natural' or is there at least some part of it for which people are responsible? Or was it perhaps entirely the result of human error or irresponsibility? If it could have been avoided, why wasn't it? Was it anything to do with not enough money or care being spent on safety or prevention?
- If there are aspects to it for which people are responsible, does this mean that any of the following are at fault (i.e. 'wrong'): one person, several people, the 'authorities' (this often means the local council), a company, several companies, a minister, a government department?
- If people are at fault, what should happen? Should they be brought to court? If they are brought to court is there a fair trial? If they are found guilty, what should happen to them? Does this happen?
- Immediately following the disaster, were things done properly? If not, why not? Was this anything to do with money or crisis management? Who should have done things properly?
- As time goes on, are the victims of the disaster treated well or badly? If not, why not? Was this anything to do with money? Who should have been looking after those affected? What is the right way to treat victims of a disaster?
- Who behaved well? Should they be rewarded? Does the way they behaved offer any pointers as to how we might all behave in ordinary times?

Think about

Research a disaster that has happened locally or anywhere in the world and think about how the points were dealt with. Some international examples are:

The Bhopal disaster – gas leak at the Union Carbide India Ltd pesticide plant in Bhopal, Madhya Pradesh, in India in 1984.

Hurricane Katrina – the extremely destructive tropical storm that hit the Gulf Coast of the United States in 2005.

The Exxon Valdez disaster – the 1989 oil spill from the oil tanker Exxon Valdez that caused what is considered to be one of the most devastating human-caused environmental disasters.

The Grenfell Tower fire

All these issues came up after a disaster that happened in West London in June 2017.

There was a fire at a tower block in which 71 people are known to have died. The fire ran through the whole block – Grenfell Tower – and everyone had to leave their homes. It was one of the worst fire disasters that has ever happened in the UK.

Immediately, the survivors started asking some of the questions on the list on page 42. And this was followed up by commentators in the media.

People wanted to know things like:

- How did the fire start?
- Was there anything in how the building was made which meant that the fire spread so quickly?
- Were there combustible materials in the building that were chosen because they were cheaper?
- Had the council listened to the people living in the block when they had raised concerns about fire safety?
- Had the authorities taken note of what had happened when fires in other tower blocks broke out? If not, why not?
- Did the fire service have all the right equipment to fight the fire and rescue people? If not, why not?
- Were the survivors treated properly? Were they found places to stay straightaway? Were they found long-term places to stay within reach of the community? If not, why not?

It was immediately clear that many of the survivors, people in the neighbourhood, and the survivors' families, did all they could to help anyone in difficulty. Some commentators said that this showed the 'good' side to people, that human beings have this quality of being able to be kind, to help and co-operate for the general good.

Does a disaster like the Grenfell Tower fire make us think about our values more closely? Do people responding to a disaster act consciously according to their values or do they act spontaneously?

Volunteers sort donations of food and clothing to help people who had to flee their homes in the wake of the Grenfell Tower fire.

What are your values?

This book raises questions to do with right and wrong, and asks you to come up with opinions and thoughts of your own. Perhaps you did this as you read it, or while you discussed it with others.

Always keep in mind that right and wrong can be very complex. And it's the questions we ask ourselves that are often just as important as the answers. Questions can prompt discussion which can lead to change.

Did you change your mind?

While you were reading, thinking and talking, did you change your mind about anything? Why was that? Do you think there's anything you've read, or any conversation you've had about what you've read, that will make you behave differently or do something new? Why is that?

Several people in the book have talked about what might be called their 'core values'. That's the main principles which guide them in their daily lives, their work, the way they vote or the kinds of clubs, societies or religious institutions they belong to.

The Golden Rule

Remember the Golden Rule that we mentioned early on? One example of it that you may have heard is 'Love thy neighbour'. People usually take this to mean 'be good and kind and caring to the person nearest to you'. And in turn, this has been taken to mean that if we all do that, society as a whole – and indeed the world – will get better.

What do you think of this principle? Would it work? Why might it not work? Can you think of a better principle?

"The strongest democracies flourish from frequent and lively debate, but they endure when people of every background and belief find a way to set aside smaller differences in service of a greater purpose."

Barack Obama

THiNK about

What principles and values do you think can best convey your own ideas about right and wrong?

Your 'volcano bag'

To help you make a list of the values that are important to you, you could think of this: there was a volcano (above) on the island of Montserrat in the Caribbean. Many people had to leave the island when it erupted. One woman who stayed was asked what she would do if she heard the volcano rumbling. She said that she had a 'volcano bag' hanging by her front door. In the bag were the things that mattered to her most: souvenirs from her family, and from her own life.

You could say that we all have a mental volcano bag: the important things that we carry with us which guide us through life – especially for when our personal volcano blows up. The people in Grenfell Tower and nearby experienced something just like that. And in their mental 'volcano bag' they had something like 'help each other' as a basic 'right thing to do'.

You could talk or write about what you think is in your own mental volcano bag.

"Democratic dissent is not disloyalty, it is a positive civic duty."

Shami Chakrabarti

What can we do to bring about what we believe is right?

Much harder, but just as necessary, is the question, 'What can we, as individuals or as members of a society or community, do to change those things we see as wrong or unjust?'.

We know that in every corner and walk of life, in every place of work, there are problems. This is just another way of saying that the question of right and wrong crops up everywhere.

But what do we do about these things? Moan to ourselves? Complain to others in the hope that they will do something? Write a letter to the person you think is responsible, or to the newspaper or television programme? Go to see your MP, a lawyer, a religious person? Do you take part by joining an association, an organisation, a protest group or a political party?

If you live in the UK you'll know that you can do any of these things and they might have the result you want. In some countries you're not allowed to do these things. Some problems are bigger than just our neighbourhood or even our country – things like climate change.

THiNK about

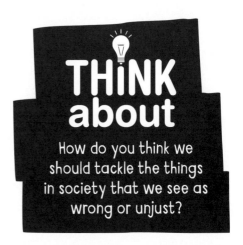

How do you think we should tackle the things in society that we see as wrong or unjust?

Glossary

apartheid the former political system in South Africa, based on racial segregation, in which only white people had full political rights and others, especially black people, were forced to live separately with inferior facilities

carbon emissions the carbon dioxide produced by cars (and by planes and factories etc), which is harmful to the environment

civic life people's public life concerned with the affairs of the community or country, in contrast to their personal life

civil rights rights designed to protect individuals from unfair treatment and to ensure they receive equal treatment, free from discrimination

communism a political system in which all property is owned and controlled by all the members of a community and everyone works as much as they can and receives what they need

conscription the process of forcing someone by law to serve in one of the armed forces

constitution the set of political principles and rights – usually written – by which a state or organisation is governed, especially in relation to the rights of the people it governs

democracy a system of government based on the belief in freedom and equality between people, in which power is either held by elected representatives or directly by the people themselves

dictator a leader of a country, who has not been elected by the people and who has complete power

discrimination treating a person or particular group of people differently – usually unfavourably – because of their skin colour, sex, sexuality, etc

elite the most powerful, and usually the richest and best-educated, group in a society

empathise to be able to understand how someone else feels

feminism the belief that women should be allowed the same rights, power, and opportunities as men and be treated in the same way

global warming Earth's rising surface temperature and its effects, such as melting glaciers and the subsequent rise in sea levels

humanists people who believe that people's spiritual and emotional needs can be met without following a god or religion

hybrid cars cars that can run on either electricity or petrol

justice fairness in the way people are dealt with, often in relation to the law

justice system the system in a society in which people who are accused of crimes are judged in a court of law

pragmatism a practical approach to dealing with problems in a way that suits the conditions that actually exist, rather than following fixed ideas or rules

prejudice an unreasonable and unfair opinion about a person or group, especially when formed without enough thought or knowledge

revolution a change in the political system of a country, often brought about by violence or war

rule of law a set of laws that people in a society must obey

tertiary education education at college or university level

theologians people who study religion and religious belief

tolerance a willingness to accept behaviour and beliefs that are different from your own, even if you do not agree with or approve of them

United Nations (UN) an international organisation that was established in 1945 and aims to solve world problems in a peaceful way. UN resolutions are an official decision voted on by the UN

universal adult suffrage the right for all adults to vote with no restriction by race, sex, belief, wealth, or social status

Further information

Here are some books and websites you might find interesting:

Books

Everyday Sexism, and *Girl Up* by Laura Bates (Simon and Schuster)

Liccle Bit, *Crongton Knights* and *Straight Outta Crongton* by Alex Wheatle (Little, Brown)

The Panchatantra by Vishnu Sharma (Penguin Books)

Aesop's Fables by Michael Rosen (Tradewind)

The Wrong Side of Right by Jenn Marie Thorne (Dial)

Young Citizen's Passport (England and Wales, Northern Ireland, and Scotland) published by the Citizenship Foundation

The Story of Ruby Bridges by Robert Coles (Scholastic)

The Island by Armin Greder (Allen and Unwin)

Noughts and Crosses by Malorie Blackman (Corgi)

The Trap, *Raining Fire* and *End Game* by Alan Gibbons (Orion Children's Books)

The Little Book of Thunks by Ian Gilbert (Crown House Publishing)

Websites

The Citizenship Foundation http://www.citizenshipfoundation.org.uk. They say:

"We help young people to understand the law, politics and democratic life... We want society to be fairer, more inclusive and more cohesive. We want a democracy in which everyone has the knowledge, skills, and confidence to take part as effective citizens."

openDemocracy https://www.opendemocracy.net. They say:

"Through reporting and analysis of social and political issues, openDemocracy seeks to challenge power and encourage democratic debate across the world. With human rights as our central guiding focus, we ask tough questions about freedom, justice and democracy."

Amnesty International https://www.amnesty.org.uk. They say:

"We work to protect women, men and children wherever justice, freedom, truth and dignity are denied. As a global movement of over 7 million people, Amnesty International is the world's largest grassroots human rights organisation. We investigate and expose abuses, educate and mobilise the public, and help transform societies to create a safer, more just world. We received the Nobel Peace Prize for our life-saving work."

How to get involved

Once you have decided on your personal values, you might want to think about how you could express these values. You could join the youth section of an organisation such as a political party or a pressure group that campaigns for issues you are interested in. Or closer to home, you could join the student council at your school.

Index

What is Right & Wrong? Who Decides? Where do Values come from? And other Big Questions

Michael Rosen & Annemarie Young

WAYLAND
www.waylandbooks.co.uk

For Emma, Elsie and Emile (M.R.)
In memory of my brother, Robert Young, who always did what he believed to be right, whatever the cost to himself (A.Y.)

First published in Great Britain in 2018 by Wayland
Michael Rosen and Annemarie Young have asserted their rights to be identified as the Author of this Work.

Editor: Nicola Edwards
Design: Rocket Design (East Anglia) Ltd
Artwork by Oli Frape
ISBN 978 1 5263 0494 0
10 9 8 7 6 5 4 3 2 1

MIX
Paper from responsible sources
FSC® C104740

Wayland, an imprint of
Hachette Children's Group
Part of Hodder and Stoughton
Carmelite House
50 Victoria Embankment
London EC4Y 0DZ

An Hachette UK Company
www.hachette.co.uk
www.hachettechildrens.co.uk

Printed and bound in China

We would like to thank:
Laura Bates, Richard Rieser, Tulip Siddiq and Alex Wheatle for sharing their experiences with us. All those who have contributed to the book in some way. Professor Jane Heal, University of Cambridge and Fellow of the British Academy, for her incisive and helpful comments on a draft of the text.
And a big thank you to our excellent editor, Nicola Edwards, for her invaluable input, as always.

Picture acknowledgements:
Back cover (left) Courtesy of Goldsmiths, University of London, (right) Anthony Robinson; p4 Shutterstock.com; p5 (clockwise from top left): © Claude Schneider; © Walter White; © Jon Armstrong; Richard Rieser; br Wikimedia Commons; p6 Courtesy of Goldsmiths, University of London; p7 Wikimedia Commons; p8t Anthony Robinson, b Wikimedia Commons; p13 Wikimedia Commons; p14 and p15t (backgrounds) Shutterstock.com; p14 Shutterstock.com; p15 (both) Wikimedia Commons; p17 Wikimedia Commons; p19 Adam Kliczek/Wikimedia Commons; p21 Sergey Kohl / Shutterstock.com; p22 Richard Rieser; p24 nikolpetr / Shutterstock.com; p25 Shutterstock.com; p27 Igor Grochev / Shutterstock.com; p28 © Jon Armstrong; p29 A. Ricardo / Shutterstock.com; p30 Shutterstock.com; p32 © Claude Schneider; p33 Michael Candelori / Shutterstock.com; p34 Shutterstock.com; p35 Shutterstock.com; p37 Wikimedia Commons; p39 Wikimedia Commons; p40 © Walter White; p43 Wikimedia Commons; p45 Shutterstock.com

Contents

What is this book about?

Every day we make decisions that are underpinned by our ideas of what is right and wrong. But where do these ideas come from? Where do our values come from and who decides which values are used in a society? This book is not going to tell you what to think. Our aim is to get you to think for yourselves about these and many other, related questions.

We think it's important that everyone should think about life's big questions, and never just accept what they are told. This doesn't mean that you can't continue to hold the ideas or values that you had, but if you do, you'll know that those values are your own and not just an unthinking acceptance of someone else's ideas.

How does the book work?

We've chosen topics that are strongly connected to the values people hold and to their ideas of what is right and wrong, such as democracy, justice, fairness, prejudice and discrimination, education, climate change and war. We'll give you information about each topic and ask questions related to them to get you thinking about your own values.

Of course, we couldn't possibly fit into this one book all the information you need in order to answer all the questions. Instead, we'll provide you with information about some key principles and institutions – such as the rule of law, and the key principles of democracy – and other aspects of the questions, such as information on wars or climate change.

How can the problems of pollution and climate change be solved? When air pollution in cities is often too bad for schoolchildren to play outside, should governments ban the combustion engine and phase in electric cars?

We'll also ask you to find out more about some of the issues and how they relate to your life and your values. For example, if your country went to war, would you take part? If your country was invaded, would you resist?

The people in the book

We'll tell you about ourselves, and how we developed our own ideas and values. You will also hear from four people – Laura Bates, Richard Rieser, Tulip Siddiq and Alex Wheatle – who'll discuss their own experiences and thoughts about right and wrong. In addition, there are quotes from other people spread through the book.

"To be neutral in a situation of injustice is to have chosen sides already. It is to support the status quo."

Archbishop Desmond Tutu

Laura Bates

Alex Wheatle

Richard Rieser

Tulip Siddiq

At the end

On the last two pages, we'll ask you to reflect on what you've read, and on the discussions you've had while reading the book. We'll ask:

- Did you change your mind about anything?
- What principles and values do you think can best convey your ideas about right and wrong?
- What can we do to bring about what we believe is right?

My experience

Michael Rosen

Michael Rosen was born in 1946. He's a writer for adults and children, a broadcaster and Professor of Children's Literature at Goldsmiths, University of London.

Ideals

Every one of us has an idea of what the words 'right' and 'wrong' mean. The ideas about 'right' are sometimes called 'ideals'. This means they are ideas about the best ways to behave, although we may not always be able to live up to them.

We may not be able to write down all our ideas about right and wrong, but we have another way of expressing right and wrong – through our actions. Sometimes what we say is right or wrong and what we actually do are different. People call this 'hypocritical' which is itself often described as 'wrong'.

For example, when I was at school, I would have said that bullying is wrong and yet sometimes I teased people in a bullying sort of a way. Then I changed schools, someone teased me, and I hated it. This showed me I had been hypocritical. It showed me that something I had done was wrong and I tried to change. If I heard myself being like that I tried to check myself but it hasn't always worked. This tells me several things about right and wrong: it's a complicated mix of 'ideals' and actions; we can learn from experience; it's not easy to live up to ideals, but for the sake of equality and fairness, it's better to try than not try.

Where do ideas about right and wrong come from?

As you're reading this, you could ask yourself, 'Where do I get my ideas about right and wrong from?'

When I ask myself this, I can see that to start off with, the biggest influence on my life was my parents. When they were children, they were very poor but they studied hard and both of them became teachers. They rejected the religion of their grandparents and tried to work out their own 'universal' principles: things like, all people should be equal, people shouldn't exploit each other or discriminate against each other, and people have the right to build this equal world. That was the 'ideal'. The big problem for them was that in countries where some leaders said they were building this new 'right' society, they were exploiting and discriminating all over again!

In the 1960s in Selma, Alabama, people marched in support of equal voting rights for black people in the USA.

As I was growing up

As I was growing up, they told me about all this.

In 1960 I was 14, so the 1960s covered my late teens and early twenties. It was just when the world was in ferment about civil rights, feminism, war, work, poverty, inequality, domination of one set of countries over other countries.

At school and university, I loved having conversations about all this. We talked about the rights and wrongs of education, work, society and war. I went to meetings and conferences and took part in demonstrations. I went to see plays, listened to music (songs, mostly) that talked of these things and I studied writers and thinkers.

I argued with my parents about some of this. Sometimes I influenced them, sometimes they influenced me. I was very lucky: even though we argued, they loved me and I loved them. And here I am, helping to write a book about right and wrong, inviting you to think and talk about it! I like to think they would think that was 'right'. This tells me that love has a lot to do with right and wrong, too.

"... love has a lot to do with right and wrong."

THiNK about

Talk to your parents or other people at home about their ideas of right and wrong. What are they and where did your parents get them from?

My experience

Annemarie Young

Annemarie Young was born in 1950. She was a publisher, and she now writes stories and information books for children and young people.

My parents' influence

My earliest ideas about right and wrong came from my parents, particularly from my mother, who was very clear about her notions of justice and fairness and right or wrong, especially in our treatment of others. My father shared her fundamental values, but they sometimes disagreed on details, and when they did, their discussions were always interesting!

My parents' values were reinforced by the nuns at school. Many of those ideals were positive and sensible: being kind to others, especially those less fortunate, doing no harm (the Golden Rule, see page 12).

But as I got older I found that other ideas and practices – for example ones that implied women were secondary to men – contradicted what I believed to be right. I began to question other Catholic teachings and finally realised that I was a humanist and didn't believe in religion.

Another influence was being the child of immigrant parents. I grew up feeling very much an outsider, and this made me empathise with those treated as the 'other'.

Witnessing injustice

On a trip from Australia to Europe in 1970, my parents were shocked by the day-to-day manifestations of apartheid in Durban in South Africa, where the ship briefly docked. They were appalled at the 'Whites Only' benches and the inferior facilities reserved for 'Blacks'.

This was one of the signs used in apartheid-era South Africa.

However, my father couldn't believe that his beloved adopted country, Australia, could also be racist. I had to convince him that parts of the White Australia policy (see panel) still existed. He also found my descriptions of government policies on Aboriginal people hard to believe because they were so blatantly unjust.

Campaigning for justice

My sense of fairness and justice developed into a belief that I should actively campaign for justice. I started by supporting groups against apartheid in South Africa and those seeking justice for Aboriginal people in Australia. Then I joined the campaign against the Vietnam War, particularly Australia's role in it.

My values continued to develop as I grew older. Many experiences reinforced my notions of justice. Once, while I was living in China in 1983, an open truck drove past full of men with crosses marked on the backs of their shaved heads. I was told they were being taken for public execution. I still shudder at the image. I believe the death penalty is always wrong, that it is state-sanctioned murder. Worst of all, what if an executed person turns out to be innocent?

> "My values continued to develop as I grew older."

The White Australia policy

Australia's long-term immigration policies effectively barred people of non-European descent from entering the country. Things slowly changed from 1949 until the Racial Discrimination Act of 1975 made racially-based selection unlawful.

The Stolen Generations

Between 1910-1970, the government forcibly removed many Aboriginal children from their families 'for their own good'– these children are known as the Stolen Generations. This racist and inhumane policy was based on the assumption of the superiority of white culture.

Putting values into practice

I now write books with my husband, Anthony Robinson, to give a voice to children who are usually not heard. We have written books in which refugee children, street children, and young Palestinians living under occupation in the West Bank, tell their stories.

I don't always live up to my own ideals, but I try! For me, the most important issue is identifying unfairness and injustice and determining what I can do to combat them, while recognising that we cannot do everything for everyone.

What do we mean by right and wrong?

Principles – what we think is 'right'

When we use the word 'right' in this book, we are talking about what are called principles or ideals. These are the rules and conventions we develop to help us run our lives. When we think these rules and conventions have been broken, we say this is wrong.

This makes it sound very simple. It's not. Consider this, for example: if I was a political leader, I might say that it's 'right' that in my country – Happyland – we need to get rid of all left-handed people. If enough people agreed with me, I could become the President and pass a law to stop left-handed people getting certain jobs. Left-handed people might say that this was unfair and protest. I might then say they were dangerous and jail or exile them. All the time I would be saying that what I was doing was 'right'.

The idea of discriminating against left-handed people might not seem very reasonable to us now, but it could work like this: a group of people with a set of beliefs, including that left-handedness is 'evil', gain enough supporters to elect the leader of the country, and that leader can then make laws based on those beliefs.

Are there any principles that are right or wrong whatever the circumstances?

It's clear from the fictional example that we can't easily say it's absolutely the case that something is right or wrong. It's obvious that not everyone in Happyland would agree with a law to stop left-handed people from getting good jobs. Many people, and not just those who are left-handed, would think it was quite unfair. The idea of fairness is very important in determining the principles we live by. We'll look at fairness in more detail later.

As you can see, people don't always agree on what is right and wrong, fair or unfair, and therefore on how we should organise and run our lives.

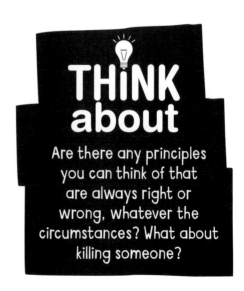

THINK about

Are there any principles you can think of that are always right or wrong, whatever the circumstances? What about killing someone?

Principles – personal and social

Ideas about right and wrong are learned through a mix of social interaction – how we interact with other people – and what we hear, read and see around us.

It's important to remember that these ideas aren't just personal, like say, whether it's right to boast about yourself. They are also social, like how we build and maintain relationships, families, communities, society and, ultimately, the whole world.

So, taking that in order, questions of right and wrong can be about, for example, whether both people in a relationship have an equal voice; whether the males and females in a family unit do equal amounts of work; what's right and wrong for our street, schools, hospitals, villages, towns and cities, and the environment; what's best for the country we live in and what's best for the world. In effect, what is best for the greatest number of people, not just for the individual.

'The greatest happiness of the greatest number' was an idea first put forward by the philosopher and legal and social reformer Jeremy Bentham (1748-1832). This became the foundation of many of our morals and legislation.

However, none of this is simple or straightforward!

THINK about

Should or could all harmful drugs, including nicotine and alcohol, be banned or regulated?

What might seem to be right for me as an individual might not be right for my neighbour, or what's right for my town might not be right for the people living in the next town. What seems to be right for my country might not be right for the world. We have to work these things out using systems of 'governance' such as councils, parliaments and international forums like the United Nations.

Government or the individual?

Governments already ban or regulate certain things that are harmful – for example, weapons, certain drugs and driving speeds. Some drugs, like cocaine, are illegal, but that doesn't stop some people from using them. Similarly, knowing that long-term misuse of some legal drugs, such as nicotine (cigarettes) and alcohol, is harmful doesn't stop some people misusing them, even though this often causes serious physical and mental health issues.

Do you think that it's up to the individual to decide if it's right or wrong to take drugs? You might like to consider the fact that illegal drugs are trafficked, distributed and sold by criminals, and that excessive drug taking and drinking of alcohol affects society and those closest to the user.

Where do values come from?

For thousands of years, all over the world, the main way people learned about right and wrong was through the sacred texts of their religions, including (in alphabetical order), Buddhism, Christianity, Hinduism, Islam, Judaism and books written by religious thinkers and leaders. At the same time – and now more so than ever – people have developed ideas about right and wrong with very little or no reference to a god or sacred texts, believing that morality comes out of human experience and personal honesty and responsibility.

The people who've written about these ideas might be philosophers, politicians, thinkers, writers and teachers like Confucius, Mary Wollstonecraft, Karl Marx, Maya Angelou and thousands of others.

However, there is one basic principle that underlies humanism and also seems to be universal to all traditions – religious and philosophical. This is known as the Golden Rule:

> 'Treat other people in the way you would like to be treated yourself.'
>
> The Golden Rule

One among many

How does the Golden Rule work? Here's a way of thinking about it: you are an individual and yet you are always in a relationship with other people who influence what you think about right and wrong – at home, at school, around your local neighbourhood and when you travel away from home. You read news reports and hear about wars, disasters, famines, diseases, great achievements and much more, and this too has an influence on your ideas about right and wrong.

One way to help ourselves sort this difficult matter out is to look around at the world and at history.

Values are not fixed

Once we do this, the first thing we notice is that ideas about what is right and wrong are not 'fixed'. For example, if you go back to, let's say, 1800 in Britain and America, you would find that many white people thought that slavery was right because white people, they would have said, were superior to black people. When you read what people said and did in the past or you look around the world, you can find examples of people saying that:

- men are superior to women,
- gay people should be put in prison,
- murderers should be executed in public.

Such ideas become more than just ideas when they are made into laws. Laws are the way in which a society or country puts into practice what a government has decided is right or wrong. This is called the 'justice system' and you can see the police, the law courts, prisons and the government all involved in this. Again, we have to remember that though at any given moment this system is all in place and settled, over time it changes and it varies from country to country.

How are values changed?

This reminds us that, in our world, these matters are set up by people expressing themselves through politics. Over time this has happened as a result of elections, demonstrations, rebellions, revolutions and wars. For example, go back to 1800 in Britain and very few people were allowed to vote. That was thought by those in power to be right. It took the actions and changing opinions of many people to alter that situation. Many people were put in prison and some people died trying to win votes for all adults.

THiNK about

Is it better to wait for those in power to change their minds? Or should we take action to change opinions and policy?

> "Men make the moral code and they expect women to accept it."
>
> Emmeline Pankhurst

Emmeline Pankhurst, founder of the Women's Social and Political Union, was arrested several times during her fight to win the right for women to vote.

What is society?

Is it like a machine?

We all live in a 'society'. This doesn't simply mean that we live in a country or nation. Some people say that 'society' is like a machine, where the parts are meshed together, each part having an effect on another one. If society was a car, you could see how turning the steering wheel makes the front wheels move. So for instance, in a society, farmers rear cattle which produce milk, which is bought by shops and supermarkets, where we then buy the milk. Over time, this becomes the 'right' way to do things.

This way of describing society suggests it all works in 'harmony', like a choir singing in tune together.

Or is society more complex and intertwined?

Another way of describing society says that, yes, we are all meshed together but the result is not fair. And this is not 'right'. You may hear on the news that the 'economy is doing well' and yet millions of people might say at the same time that they are poorer, that the economy is not doing well for them, and that this is not 'right'. This suggests that the idea of society as a machine doesn't paint the whole picture. The car might be going forward but it's left some of the passengers behind!

Then again, people say that when the 'economy is doing well' some people are indeed doing very well. How come? Is it because they work harder, or they are cleverer, or what? And is this right?

Maybe, say some, it's not so much that the passengers are left behind, rather that they are pushing the car along so that one or two people can sit in the car! If that describes the situation, would that be right?

How do societies change?

Let's stay with cars for the time being. Over time, they have changed and many more people have them. Some people think this is good and right. They say it's 'progress'. Others say that all these cars have ended up causing accidents, deaths and pollution: not so right.

There are two views of how society changes. One view is that we are generally getting better and better at getting things right for more and more people: we live longer, we are better at airing our views, there is less discrimination, even the poorest are better off than the poorest of a hundred years ago, we are wiping out diseases, more people are better educated than ever before. This suggests that society is like a line on a graph going up, getting better and better.

Another view is that while some things are better, other things get worse. In other words, some things (like advances in medicine, the invention of labour-saving devices and votes for all) are right and some things, like wars, terrorism, inequality, pollution, famine and climate change are wrong. Perhaps the graph looks more like a spiral going forwards and up and curving back down!

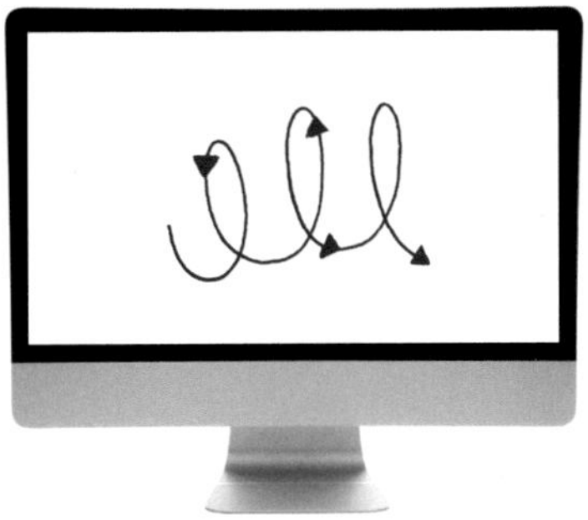

The spiral society: while technological advances in transport have connected people and places like never before, roads have become increasingly congested and dangerous and the air ever more polluted.

Where are we now on the line or spiral?

Are we on the line going up or are we in a spiral? If it's the line, then we don't have to do anything different from what we're doing now. If it's the spiral then we have to come up with ideas for how to stop that 'curving back down' effect. This is exactly where our different ideas about right and wrong come in.

THiNK about

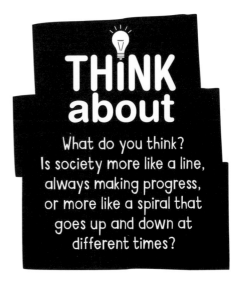

What do you think? Is society more like a line, always making progress, or more like a spiral that goes up and down at different times?

What is democracy?

There are some forms of government where power is held by one person, as in dictatorships, or by a small number of individuals, like army generals or tribal leaders – and where the people have no real say in how the government works, or in replacing the government with another.

In contrast, democracy is based on the belief in freedom and equality between people. It describes a system of government in which power is usually held by representatives who are elected by a majority of those eligible to vote. There are almost as many different ways of organising this system as there are democratic countries.

What happens when people disagree with laws?

Democratic societies allow people to protest and argue against laws they disagree with. As we've seen, ideas of what is fair and just change and it's often the case that changes in laws come about through protest as well as debate (see page 13).

Democracy requires compromise - groups with different interests and opinions must be willing to negotiate with each other.

In a democracy, one group does not always win everything it wants. Different combinations of groups win on different issues. But if one group is always excluded and fails to be heard, it may turn against democracy in anger and frustration, leading to civil unrest.

Key principles of a democracy

- A political system for choosing and replacing a government through regular elections that are free and fair.
- A government is chosen by a majority of the people, but the rights of those who voted for the opposition are respected, and the rights of minorities are protected in various ways.
- The active participation of the people in what is called 'civic life'.
- The protection of the human rights of all citizens, including freedom of expression.
- Freedom of the press and media, without interference from the state.
- The 'rule of law' (see page 18), which applies equally to all citizens.
- There are limits to what the government can do, based on a constitution, (not necessarily written) or other charter that sets out basic principles.
- There are a number of different groups or parties, with different views, and there isn't one elite or group of elites that effectively have the power.
- It is based on the values of tolerance, pragmatism, cooperation and compromise.

More titles in the **... And other big questions** series

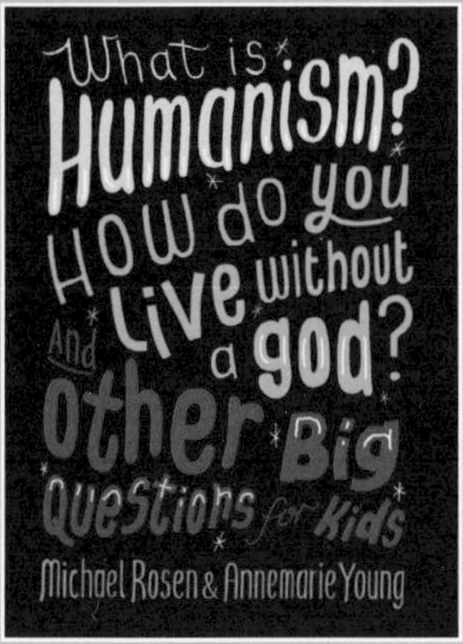

What Is Humanism?

9780750288422
(PB Edition)

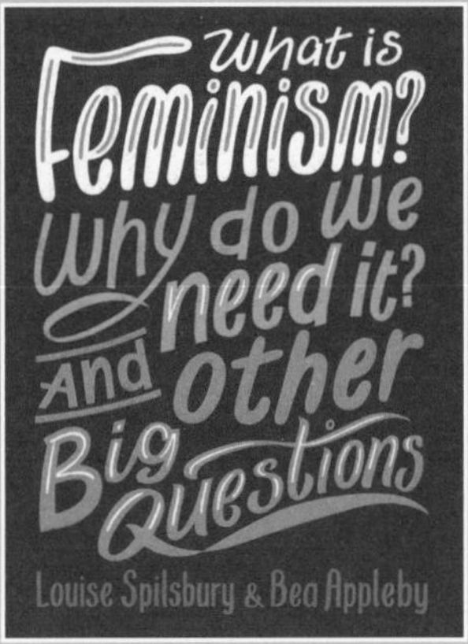

What Is Feminism?

9780750298377

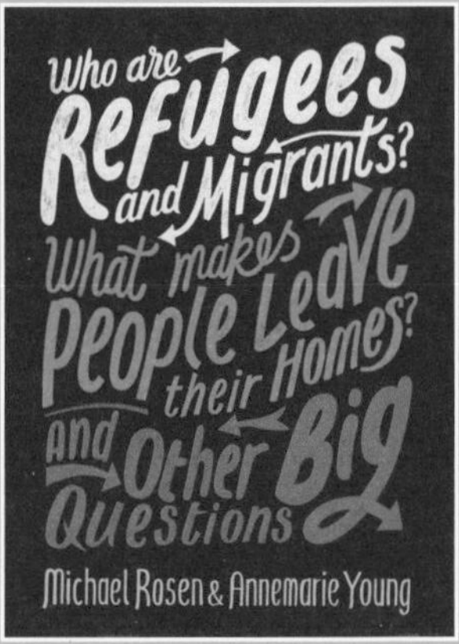

Who Are Refugees and Migrants?

9780750299855

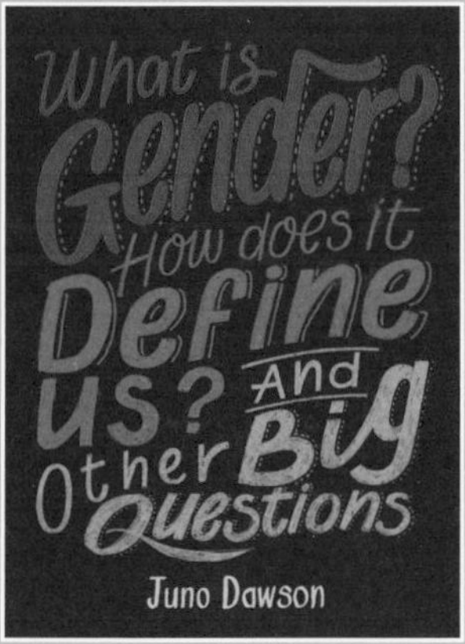

What Is Gender?

9781526300003

What Is Consent?

9781526300911

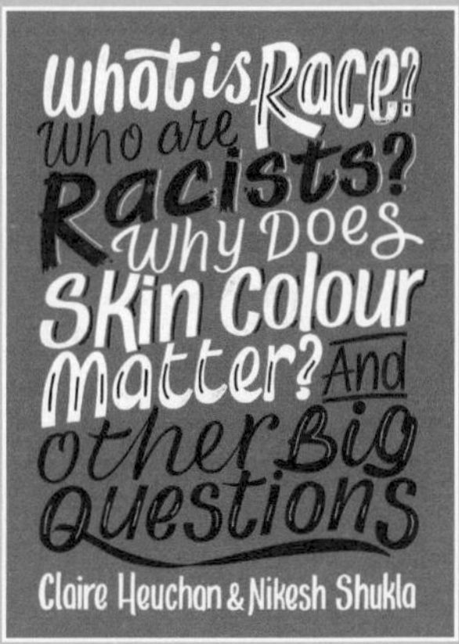

What is Race?

9781526303981